GREGORIO ESPARZA

✯ Alamo Hero ✯

GREGORIO ESPARZA

✶ Alamo Hero ✶

By
Cahndice Matthews

EAKIN PRESS ★ Austin, Texas

Library of Congress Cataloging-in-Publication Data:

Matthews, Cahndice.
  Gregorio Esparza : Alamo hero / by Cahndice Matthews.
  j.   cm.
  Includes bibliographical references (p.   ).
  ISBN 1-57168-061-6
  1. Esparza, Gregorio, 1808–1836 — Juvenile literature. 2. Alamo (San
Antonio, Tex.) — Siege, 1836 — Biography — Juvenile literature. 3. Pioneers
— Texas — Biography — Juvenile literature. I. Title.
  F390.E87M38   1996
  976.4'03'092--dc20
  [B]   95-36585
                                                                      CIP
                                                                       AC

*This work is dedicated to
the defenders of the Alamo,
the student body at
Gregorio Esparza Elementary,
and to my husband, Troy,
for always believing in me,
and to David, my son,
for his patience.*

CONTENTS

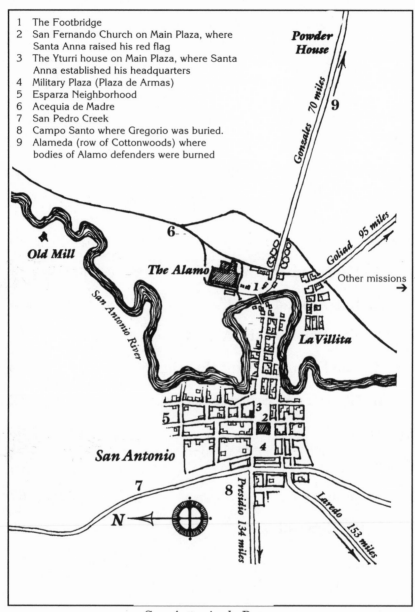

1 The Footbridge
2 San Fernando Church on Main Plaza, where
   Santa Anna raised his red flag
3 The Yturri house on Main Plaza, where Santa
   Anna established his headquarters
4 Military Plaza (Plaza de Armas)
5 Esparza Neighborhood
6 Acequia de Madre
7 San Pedro Creek
8 Campo Santo where Gregorio was buried.
9 Alameda (row of Cottonwoods) where
   bodies of Alamo defenders were burned

*San Antonio de Bexar
during Gregorio Esparza's life
courtesy Docu Tex Press*

PREFACE

Texans had many unsung heroes at the Battle of the Alamo, who fought and died for the state's freedom from Mexico. Among those were ten men with Spanish surnames and some of their families. This is the story of one of them — Gregorio Esparza — and the events surrounding his service to Texas.

I wish to express my thanks to Melva Matkin, principal at Esparza Elementary, Mary Alice Ramirez, Yvonne Dilley-Cruz, and the entire Esparza faculty and staff for their anticipation of "our" book, and their confidence in my ability to do it justice. A special thanks goes to Rey and Nora Esparza and Lena Olivares not only for extending to me their immeasurable hospitality, but also for entrusting me with a part of Gregorio Esparza through invaluable interviews, priceless photographs, and thought-provoking articles that made this work truly special.

CHAPTER ONE

Early Life of Gregorio

*T*he wheels on the small wagon came to a screeching, slow stop. The old man rested the leather reins of the ox in the wooden seat. He stepped down onto the dry, foreign soil and looked around him. The trip had been a long one from Saltillo, Mexico. He was happy to be here.

What Grandpa Jose Esparza saw before him was not what he had been told about or expected.

He lifted the sombrero from his crown and wiped his dusty, parched face with a fringed edge of his serape. He looked out across the valley for the Plaza de las Islas, named for his Canary Island ancestors who had started San Antonio de Bexar.

At first he was disappointed. There had been slow growth in Bexar's population after approximately 1790, because of laws to get land, relations with the Indians, and racial beliefs.

A short distance away, he could see something familiar to him — a cross, rising slightly above the other buildings around it. This church, named San Fernando, was the first building constructed by the Canary Islanders, in July of 1731. The center point of the front doors at

1

San Fernando was used for laying out the city. The church would serve the Esparzas for many years to come.

Grandpa Jose made the sign of the cross over his chest and thanked God for his safe trip.

The Esparza family moved to the area of San Antonio de Bexar in 1795. The family descended from the Canary Islanders, some of the first European families to move to Texas.

The Esparzas were part of the first *"entradas"* into Texas from Mexico. At San Pedro Springs they started their first settlement of families whose names have lived through three centuries and are still borne by citizens of San Antonio today. The original name of Esparza came from Spain's first royal crown.

Some of the Esparza ancestors had been here forever, it seemed. They were Indians. When the European Spaniards came, and others — French Creoles, Mestizos, and Mulattos — they mixed with the native Indians. Many of the Esparzas were of mixed blood and Indian heritage.

Grandpa Jose's son, Juan Antonio Esparza, married Maria Petra Olivas at San Fernando on July 20, 1799. Jose Gregorio Esparza, known as Gregorio Esparza, was born to them in San Antonio de Bexar, New Spain, on March 11, 1808. Some records give a different date of birth, but March 11 is the date used by family members and the school that was later named for this Texas hero.

Gregorio was the youngest of six children. Only two brothers and one sister lived to be adults: Jose Francisco, Victor Filomelo, and Maria Josefa Esmeregilda. Maria was the oldest child from her mother's previous marriage. Twin boys were born to Juan and Maria in 1802: Antonio Thomas Sesario and Jose Maria Sesario, sometimes recorded as Juan Nepomunceno. San Fernando Church burial records show that both died as children. Antonio

2

died first, at five months of age. Then Jose, at a year and ten months.

The Esparza family was poor, but they worked hard together to make a good life for themselves. They lived north of Main Plaza. The house had a fireplace and chimney. The fireplace was a smoky one, so Maria, Gregorio's mother, cooked outside most of the time. The mild winters in San Antonio made it possible for the Esparzas to sleep on rawhides and eat outdoors often.

Juan hunted, fished, and farmed to feed his family. The church gave them some rich land not far from the mission called the Alamo. There they grew fruits and vegetables.

Gregorio and his brothers wore cotton shirts and pants tied together with rawhide string. They didn't have hats to cover their heads from the blazing sun, or shoes to protect their feet from the cool, muddy earth when it rained. Their parents could not afford these basic needs for the Texas climate.

Gregorio liked to swim and fish in the water of the San Antonio River, which first drew his grandfather to this valley. A few miles west, the limestone banks of the San Pedro Springs were shaded by wide oaks and pecan trees heavy with nuts.

Gregorio liked to play games with his friends using sticks and pebbles. They would draw a large circle in the dirt with a stick to mark their playing area and then shoot "marbles" that were really stones.

As a young boy, Gregorio did not go to school. He needed to help his mother and father work. When he was older, he worked as a *jornalero* farmer and did odd jobs for the priest at San Fernando, like farming and moving carts on Camino Viejo de las Carretas.

Gregorio lived all of his short life in San Antonio.

CHAPTER TWO

Life Around the Mission

The area where Gregorio lived already had a rich history by the time he was born. The settlement of San Antonio de Bexar originally had three separate societies: the Mission San Antonio de Valero, the Presidio de San Antonio, and the civilian Villa de Bexar. The Villa de Bexar was made up of El Potrero, La Villita, and four barrios. Each group tried to run on its own, putting their own needs before their neighbors. But frontier life was too hard and forced them to work together and create one working society.

In 1691 a Spanish expedition arrived at the Coahuiltecan Indian village called Yanaguana. A Mass was said, and since they had arrived on the feast day for St. Anthony they named the beautiful river there San Antonio de Padua. The Spaniards moved on, but eighteen years later a second expedition arrived near the spot. With this group was a dedicated Franciscan priest, Father Antonio Olivares. He was so impressed with the location that he asked the viceroy of Mexico for permission to establish a mission there. Father Olivares had been working with the Native Americans along the Rio Grande and had established several missions in the area.

It took Father Olivares some time, but in 1718 he was granted permission by the viceroy, Baltasar de Zuñiga, the Marquis de Valero, to establish a mission near the headwaters of the San Antonio River. At the same time the viceroy ordered the Spanish governor of Texas, Martin de Alarcon, to establish a royal presidio or garrison there.

On May 1 of that year Father Olivares transferred his staff from the mission on the Rio Grande to the new spot near the San Antonio River. He named the new mission San Antonio de Valero. He did this to honor the first name given to the area by the Spaniards (San Antonio) and to pay respect to the viceroy of Mexico.

The chosen spot was on the west side of the river. After a few years, Olivares moved the location to the east side of the river. A hurricane struck and destroyed the handful of thacket buildings. In 1724, the mission was moved again. At this location work to build permanent buildings began. There Mission Valero would stay.

One of the reasons Father Olivares liked the area was because of the San Antonio River and nearby San Pedro Creek. Good water meant that farms and ranches could be irrigated. Another reason was the Indians themselves. They were small family bands who were hunters and gatherers. History remembers them as the Coahuiltecans. They were often attacked by their neighbors, particularly the Apache.

The purpose of the mission was to convert the Native Americans to Spanish subjects and Christians. Indian quarters and workshops were built along a large open plaza. A granary to store corn and other crops was also built. The Franciscans constructed a large, two-story stone building on the east side of the plaza for themselves. This was called a *convento*. Cattle and goat pens were also built. It was very important that the mission survive on its own. So the Indians were taught how to

raise cattle, grow crops, make adobe bricks, and learn other skills. Large tracts of surrounding lands were irrigated with water ditches or *acequias*. Further away the mission had its own ranch where cattle and other animals grazed.

The Franciscans hoped that in a few dozen years the mission Indians would be able to live on their own. The mission would then become its own town, with a local government. The plaza would become the center of this town.

The most impressive feature of a mission was its church. It was to be the showplace of the new town. But the Franciscans had problems building a church. The first one collapsed. The second would never be finished.

A few years later, an epidemic left Mission Valero unfinished. Illness reduced the number of Indians in the mission from 837 to 182.

There are several stories as to how the Alamo got its name. The word *"alamo"* means "cottonwood" in Spanish. Many cottonwood trees grew along the *acequia* that flowed through the mission grounds. Some believe that these trees were the reason that the Mission San Antonio de Valero became known as the Alamo. Others think that the name was used because the mission was used to move troops from Alamo de Parras in Coahuila, Mexico, to San Antonio in 1803.

Although soldiers and others went to chapel services in the building, the mission itself was forgotten for many years. It is the only mission in Texas not known by a religious name.

Life at the mission was not easy. Everyone had a special job to do. The men worked in the fields, tended the animals, and made adobe. The christianized Indians were taken care of by the mission. They picked, gathered, and wove cloth for converts and priests. Rows of adobe houses for the Indians made a large square which the

8

acequia ran through. The women wove baskets and mats by hand. They made cloth on looms for clothing.

The Alamo had a ranch, Rancheo del Los Moras, where goats, sheep, and cattle were raised. The fields were well planted with corn, peppers, and beans for food and cotton for clothing. The women ground the corn for tortillas, gorditas, and atole. They cooked simple foods such as beans, corn, and chiles, which were eaten daily. There were oxen, plows, and carts for water and wood.

The Alamo had industries operating by 1740, or even earlier. These included a monastery with housing, a porter's lodge, and a kitchen. There were also offices with supplies that the ministers needed for their work with the Indians. The patio housed the four European-styled hand looms that the women used for weaving coarse cloth, cotton shawls, sack cloth, scarves, and blankets. In two other rooms wool, cotton cards, combs, skeins, and other materials were kept for making cloth.

The Presidio de San Antonio de Bexar was located between the San Antonio River and San Pedro Creek. There was nothing between this garrison and the Villa de San Fernando but the church. The Spanish Crown started a military garrison to protect San Antonio de Valero and the other missions (four others had been built to the south along the San Antonio River). San Antonio de Valero was surrounded by a poor stockade, mounted with a few swivel guns. There was no chaplain. The parish priest received a small pension for looking after the presidio.

The Plaza de Armas was the military center of Villa de San Fernando de Bexar and San Antonio de Bexar. A jail, barracks, captain's quarters, marketplace, and private homes formed an enclosure around a square that made up the Plaza.

Many of the soldiers who settled around the presidial compound were of mixed racial heritage. They defended the area from Indian attacks and worked the land in the area along with their families.

In 1809, the town was divided into four barrios by Governor Salcedo. Each had its own governing body: Barrio del Sur, Barrio del Norte, Barrio de Laredo, and Barrio de Valero.

At that time, the town had about 2,000 people. Most were Spaniards and Creoles. The rest were Frenchmen, Americans, and civilized Indians. In time new settlers came. There were army officers, the governor's people, and the clergy. A society began to form and grow.

Barrio de Valero's people were immigrants from the East Texas presidio Las Adaes, which the Spanish Crown had left in 1770. It was located east of the San Antonio River. Farms were shared between them and thirteen Indian families still in the Mission de Valero. Since the mission was no longer being used for religious purposes in 1773, the Spanish authorities began secularizing the mission. Barrio de Valero was home to soldiers and their families. La Villita was in Barrio de Valero.

Barrio de Laredo was located west of the San Pedro Creek. Many felt it was too far from the presidio for good protection from Indians. The "far side of the creek" was not settled for years. Then, during the 1740s and 1750s, a few people got land along the road to Laredo. In the 1760s and 1770s, when more people came, they made their homes there. When the San Fernando Church cemetery became too small, the Campo Santo was established in Barrio de Laredo in 1808.

When not living on their ranches, the community's richest citizens lived in Barrio del Norte. One of the most well-known places in this barrio was the Veramendi home on Soledad Street. At first, residents lived in the houses or barracks around the squares of the presidio and villa. Then people received *solares* for houses and orchards between the river and the creek, north of the plazas, and the community grew.

Barrio del Sur included the villa's original farmlands. Thirty-two pieces of land were given to fifteen Canary Island families and four single men. To make sure they could all get water, the land grants were given in long strips that extended from the San Antonio River to San Pedro Creek. The area was used as farmland well into the nineteenth century, when it slowly turned into neighborhoods.

Crown officials wanted more people to move in and provide more money for the area, even though the mission and presidio had a growing Spanish population along the San Antonio River. Fifty-six Canary Islanders were sought to settle in Bexar and make a formal town. Directly east and next to the presidio, the church, the city council building, and private homes made a square Plaza de las Islas.

El Potrero, located directly east of the villa, was first given to the Villa de San Fernando for pasturelands to be used by the community. It was not exactly a mission, but it had many of the mission features in its early days. It was first built in 1734 as the parish church.

Isleños made up the population. They practically had control of the whole *regimiento*. The settlers gave their word to the friars not to build too close to the mission to protect the Indians. It soon grew, though, and homesites were given out during the 1760s and 1770s.

The town had fifty-nine houses of stone and mud and seventy-nine of wood, all poorly built. It looked more like a poor village than a villa. The street Calle de los Adovitos filled with water the minute it rained. The church building was big with a high roof but was also poorly made.

The Esparza family went to church at San Fernando. Sundays were very festive. After vespers and

Mass there was a *fiesta*. They visited for a long time with family and friends. The adults danced and talked. The children played. The Indians from Mission San Jose sometimes came to Mass and the *fiesta*.

La Villita, a small neighborhood located south of the mission, was quickly becoming the center of a growing Southwest. It grew because of the secularization of the San Antonio de Valero. Life behind mission walls stayed the same with sandaled, brown-robed monks and a daily routine of ringing bells in chapel towers.

In the century after the establishment of the mission, presidio, and villa, the population of the settlement of San Antonio de Bexar changed. It was first populated by Indians, Mexican soldier-settlers, and Canary Islanders. But, by the early 1800s, the mission, presidio, and villa needed each other more and the community of San Antonio had become more integrated.

By 1811, San Antonio was not a nice place for lawful people to live. The commanding officer of the American army had left San Antonio with his officers, and the town was left with a wild bunch of troops. They took the law into their own hands.

Around the Esparza home there was much talk about the different political groups in San Antonio de Bexar. Gregorio and his brother Francisco listened as their father, Juan, and Grandpa Jose talked.

*M*ore *American prisoners are being brought to the Presidio in irons and under guard, Papa," said Juan to Grandpa Jose.*

"There's talk of trouble over the Texas and Louisiana border," Grandpa replied. "Governor Cordero has brought lots of troops through on his way to meet General Wilkinson, who is threatening the border. He has set up his home here." Grandpa Jose continued, "Who do you side with? Mexico or the Spanish Crown?"

*"Neither," Juan said. "We want freedom from Mexico
as well. Look at Gregorio and Francisco. They were born
here. They know nothing of the old country, but from the
tales of old men!"*

*Grandpa looked into the eyes of his grandsons and
sighed.*

*The Esparza brothers were growing and thinking in
different ways. Gregorio felt his father to be right. He
wanted Texas to be free from Mexico. Francisco, though,
had other ideas.*

In 1813, things began to get ugly again in San Antonio. Another bloody fight took place just south of the
Medina River. By the end of the fight, between seventy
and eighty were caught and shot. The winning general
marched into San Antonio, and the unhappy town was in
chaos again. He put 700 people in jail. Eighteen out of
300 people were placed in one house and died during the
night because of crowded conditions. Five hundred
women were put in jail and were forced to make tortillas
each day for the royal army.

By 1816, San Antonio was almost a ghost town. It had
stood for nothing but terror to its former citizens. The
street called Calle de los Amargurras was later named for
the bad things that happened on Military Plaza.

In December of 1820, Moses Austin of Connecticut
came to see Governor Martinez with an idea about bring-
ing a colony to Texas. Austin died soon after but left his
son, Stephen F., to see that his project was finished.

When the news spread of the separation of Mexico
from Spain, the people of San Antonio returned and
other people began to move to Texas. San Antonio had a
population of 5,000 by 1823.

In 1831, James Bowie and his brother Rezin P. came
looking for the mines said to be at San Saba Mission.
Gregorio became friendly with James Bowie. As a young

man now, Gregorio was taken with Bowie. He respected his Bowie knife. Bowie had no family. His wife and children had died.

Sam Houston arrived for the first time in early 1833. He met James Bowie, and they held a meeting with the Comanche chiefs to make a peace treaty. Texas was not getting along well with Mexico, of which she was a part. Stephen F. Austin went to Mexico to meet with Vice-president Gomez Farias about the problem. Angry with Austin about an earlier matter, Farias refused when Austin asked for freedom for Texas from Mexico. On his way home, Austin was arrested and jailed in Mexico.

By 1834, Antonio López de Santa Anna had come to power in Mexico. President Santa Anna, who also served as general, said he would not grant Texas her freedom. The war was about to begin.

CHAPTER THREE

The Battle at the Alamo

In the Storming of Bexar, December 5-10, 1835, some 300 Texans took over San Antonio, fighting from house to house. Mexican General Martin Perfecto de Cos, Santa Anna's brother-in-law, defended the city with 1,200 men.

The Esparza family, who had been a part of San Antonio for a long time now, became divided on this occasion. Many people supported the Constitution of 1824 but not the move for independence. Many supported Santa Anna.

Gregorio was a private in the Benavides company under Captain Juan Seguin. He was a Federalist. Federalists were a political party in early U.S. history who believed in a strong central government and a democratic constitution. In December of 1835, Gregorio's brother Francisco chose General Cos' army, the Centralists, and served in the company of Leal Presidios. Centralists believed in giving power to a few individuals or a group.

General Cos gave up on December 10, 1835. The Texans let General Cos and his men go back to Mexico as long as they promised to never fight against Texas again. Those soldiers in General Cos' army who lived in Texas were allowed to remain in Texas, so Francisco stayed in San Antonio.

As the new year rolled on, days turned to weeks, and weeks to months. It was February 1836. Gregorio, now with a wife, Ana, and children, lived some distance from the Alamo, in a house on El Calle de Acequia.

At the Alamo, Lieutenant Colonel William B. Travis and other Texans were defending the mission. Colonel Travis told James Bonham, his best horseman, to go to Goliad and bring help from Colonel James W. Fannin and his men at Fort Defiance. They knew a Mexican attack would come soon.

With *all the men of fighting age joining the war, Ana knew what the look on her husband's face meant. She worried for him and their children. Gregorio didn't know how to tell his family what he'd decided.*

Ana spoke first. "I know what you must be feeling."

"How could you, Ana? A woman doesn't know the worries of a man!" said Gregorio.

"Oh, but I do. If you do not fight Santa Anna and his men, then who will? You side with Texas. After all, this is your home, our home — Texas. But if you are killed, who will care for us, your wife and sons, the ones you promised your life to?" Ana replied.

"My dear wife, you do understand, don't you?" Gregorio asked.

"Yes, Gregorio, I do," answered Ana. Gregorio held his wife.

That day, February 23, seemed like any other. Gregorio and his friend John Smith were working beside each other when word came that Santa Anna and his men were nearing the Alamo. To see if the news was true, Gregorio and John Smith found Juan Seguin.

"Captain Seguin, we've heard the news about Santa Anna and his troops."

"Yes, Private, it is true," confirmed the captain.

"Sir, John and I would like to send our families away to safety in Nacogdoches," Gregorio requested.

17

"This is a good idea," Seguin agreed. "I will have a wagon meet your families at Camino Real at Nacog-doches. Get them ready."

It was about sundown. Gregorio's sons, Enrique and Manuel, were playing along the street, skipping stones into the acequia, when the commotion started. People ran like rats. Dust clouds rose from the thunder pounding the ground. Horses whinnied and bucked as their riders rode them four abreast and nearly 3,000 strong into San Antonio. More were on their way.

The boys rose to their feet, their mouths open, their eyes wide. Wanting to run, they couldn't move. They needed to warn their father and neighbors. The boys raced through the livestock and people.

"Is it true Santa Anna is here. . . now?" Gregorio shook Enrique for the truth. When he learned it was true, he told his wife, Ana, "You are all trapped here!"

Gathering her family together, Ana asked Gregorio, "What about the old mission? Wouldn't we be safe there?"

"Yes!" answered Gregorio. "Let's go!" He pushed his family out of their home. Outside, people running and screaming had gathered what they could in sacks and wagon beds and fled. The Esparzas had taken a few clothes and bags of food. Everything else was left. People left behind cherished family possessions and fine furnishings, out of fear for one man and his wrath, Antonio López de Santa Anna.

The Esparza family arrived at the Alamo at twilight on the first day of the siege, February 23, 1836, to bolted doors. They were too late.

"This can't be!" shouted Gregorio.

"Let us in!" Ana screamed.

"It is Esparza, with my family," Gregorio pleaded to his friends inside. "Have mercy on us. We have no place to go."

The bolted doors could not be opened for them. It was too dangerous with Santa Anna so close. Gregorio wrestled

18

with the heavy doors again and again. As panic began to overtake him, someone took a risk. The main gate on the south side was opened and the Esparzas went through. There were several others behind doors, on the roof, and in the convent.

On Gregorio's first night at the Alamo, it was pitch black. The sentinels rested from duty and all the doors were closed and barred. Those on the roof stayed protected by the walls of the Alamo church and the old convent building.

Gregorio's family was in the Alamo Chapel. There was plenty of food and water. No thanks to Santa Anna, who had cut off the way to the *acequia* to try to keep the defenders and their families from getting water. Fortunately, a well had been dug in the church. There were cattle for food. Ammunition, though, was in short supply.

Outside the mission walls, Santa Anna and his men, in full dress uniform, left their horses on Main Plaza in front of San Fernando. First used by the soldiers of Spain, then by Mexican forces, and most recently by Texans, Main Plaza became a part of the presidio where the officers had their headquarters. The Texans had left the plaza for the Alamo, which was safer.

Santa Anna gave his horse's silver bridle reins to a lackey and went into the house on the northwest corner of Main Plaza. Soon, a messenger from Santa Anna called for the Alamo defenders to give up. The Texans replied with a cannon shot from the roof of the Alamo. Cheers came from the Alamo gunners. Santa Anna answered with a shot that struck the walls of the church and convent. The red flag symbolizing "no quarter" flew from the belfry of the church in Military Plaza.

The cannon in the Alamo church and convent fired over and over as Bonham crashed through enemy lines with Mexican troops close behind. He reported that

Fannin was in no hurry to leave Goliad. When Bonham left for help, Santa Anna was thought to still be days away from San Antonio. Travis thought that once Fannin knew how much trouble the men at the Alamo were in, he would leave right away for San Antonio.

Bonham met two other messengers on his way back, taking the news to others of Santa Anna's early arrival. He learned from them that the new Texas Convention was meeting at Washington-on-the-Brazos on March 1. Santa Anna didn't know a secret trail let couriers come and go. Some twenty of them got through with messages during the siege.

Santa Anna was known for his war skills. He watched and waited, making the Texans nervous and tired. With Santa Anna in no hurry, the messengers hoped that if the Texans could fight for one week, help would come quickly from the Convention.

All made it through the first day. Night fell, and Santa Anna got his men ready to the west for the next day of fighting.

The next morning, while Travis was alone in a bare adobe room where the religious men once lived, he wrote a message to the people of the United States. The letter said, "I shall never surrender or retreat." This feeling was the same for the Texans and kept them going for a long time. He ended his letter with these words: "Victory or Death." It was sent with a messenger the next day.

On the third day, Santa Anna moved in south of the main gate and put his men by the *jacales* along the Alamo for cover. This worried the Texans. In order to keep the troops from using the *jacales*, Travis asked someone to burn the huts. They could not wait for nightfall. It had to be done right away. Two youngsters burst from the Alamo. Gunfire shot through the air as the boys went in and out each *jacal,* leaving a bonfire behind them. Going back into the safety of the Alamo, they met happy Texans who had Santa Anna's anger to deal with now. His men had been forced to fall back.

The Alamo defenders had won this time, but the job was not done. Others went out on the nights after that to burn the rest of the *jacales*. It was not easy to hide from the Mexican troops.

Each morning the Texans looked to the east for help from Fannin's troops in Goliad. But on every side were blue and red Mexican uniforms for as far as the eye could see.

The weather changed on February 27 and so did the mood of the Texas soldiers. The bitter wind that blew from the north chilled the tired Texans. Santa Anna's band from the presidio played all the time. The bugles sounded the "Degüello," the hymn of death without mercy, to keep the Texans from their sleep and to wear them down. Nerves became frayed and tempers grew short. Crockett tried to lighten things up with laughter and music, but it didn't help. Sick and unable to move from his cot, Bowie grew even sicker.

Out of a dozen or so messengers sent, none had come back. Now outnumbered fifty to one, the Texans needed help right away. Again, Bonham, the great horseman, was chosen. As a good speaker, he could tell Fannin about the need for quick action. With a white handkerchief tied to his hat so the Texans would know him when he returned, he rode away.

Two days later, Travis asked for men to go again and get help. The defenders were quiet. No one would leave. They weren't afraid to fight. They only feared being called cowards if they left now. Finally, two brave Tejano men answered the plea.

"I will go, Señor Travis," said Captain Juan Seguin as he stepped forward.

"I will go with you, Captain Seguin," Antonio Arocha stated proudly. Seguin and Arocha were Mexican and could speak Spanish. That would be in their favor if they were caught by the enemy. They were to go to Gonzales and on to the Texas Convention, set to meet the next day, 150 miles away.

At last, Bonham found Fannin and his men from Goliad. On February 28 with 400 men, they set out for San Antonio. The troops did not get far before they had troubles of their own. Three supply wagons loaded with gunpowder, which the Alamo needed badly, broke down. While camped for the night, the oxen got away while grazing. Now, trying to decide whether to keep going or turn back, word came that more of Santa Anna's army, 1,000 of them, were just two days from Goliad.

Fannin made his decision. He would not leave the fort he had named, Fort Defiance. Pulling and pushing the wagons themselves, the troops from Goliad turned back. They had their own fort to protect.

Seguin and Arocha reached Gonzales to find thirty-two men and boys who had been waiting for Fannin since February 25 to join them and go to the Alamo.

On February 29, John Smith, Gregorio's friend and messenger for Travis, guided the thirty-two men into the fort. They knew, as Gregorio had known, what their decisions to join the fighting meant. There was no chance that they and the defenders at the Alamo would beat Santa Anna, but for the sons of Texas and those who had chosen this land, it was the only choice.

On the early morning of March 1, the Texans cheered to greet who they thought were just part of Fannin's 400 men. When they realized that the thirty-two were all the help they were going to get, silence fell. Then came cheers as they knew the courage and love for their home that brought those few men to save their beloved Texas. They felt like celebrating, so a side of beef was cut and they had a barbecue.

The next morning, March 3, during a cease fire ordered by Santa Anna, Travis thought about what was going to happen to them. He drew a line on the ground with his sword and asked for those who would stay with him to step across. One hundred eighty-six men moved forward. Bowie, on his cot, and very ill, asked to be moved across to the side with the fighting men. Those who wanted to leave could, never to be looked upon badly, but with thanks for their help. One man did, Moses Rose from France. He did not share the feeling for Texas that the others had. Rose left the Alamo from a window in the church.

Travis asked his men to go down fighting with him. Nineteen were from England and other countries, a few were from the northern United States, thirty-two were from Tennessee, and other Southern states had about twelve each. Nine were Tejanos: Juan Abamillo, Juan Abadillo, Carlos Espalier, Gregorio Esparza, Antonio Fuentes, Jose Maria Guerrero, Domacio Jimenez, Toborio Losoya, and Andres Nava.

*T*he time had come for Gregorio to face his wife and children.

"Son, you are twelve years old, nearly a man now. You know that this day could be my last. If things get worse, get help from your uncles." Gregorio saw the look on his young son's face.

"Don't think badly of your Uncle Francisco because he sides with our enemy," Gregorio continued. "You are his blood. He loves you and our family. You must respect his decision to take a stand for what he thinks is right."

Enrique squeezed his father with all his might. "Yes, Papa, I will," Enrique promised.

"Gregorio, what will become of us?" Ana asked, her head on Gregorio's shoulder.

"You and the children must get out," said Gregorio. "One has already. There is still time. Several messengers have gotten through. That is what I want for you and our children."

Ana had made her decision. "I will stay by your side with our children and die too. They will soon kill us. We will not suffer."

Early on the morning of March 4 Santa Anna called a meeting of his top men to talk about attacking the Alamo. While firing all their cannons at once, the troops shattered a section of the Alamo's north wall.

At the Convention, a new provisional president, David G. Burnet, was appointed, and Sam Houston was named commander-in-chief of all Texas land forces.

By dawn on March 5, the Mexican battery from the north pushed to within 200 yards of the Alamo. The Mexicans' fire was heavy and steady.

Santa Anna gave his officers a plan for the last attack. It would be all at once from the east, south, northwest, and northeast.

That night, the general was strangely nice to his enemies. His bands stopped playing and the Texans got a few hours of sleep. The horror and terror of that scary night was too much for the women and children. There was very little food left and they were tired and hungry.

At 4:00 A.M. on Sunday March 6, the Texans awakened to a loud bugle blast, the sight of 1,800 Mexican troops inside their Alamo climbing the walls, and Santa Anna's "Degüello."

Just after 5:00 A.M., at daybreak, the Mexicans stormed forward, nearly flooding the Texans. Travis dashed from his room with his shotgun and sword and raced to his twelve-pound cannon with his slave, Joe, behind him. Crockett and his "Tennessee boys" worked the stockade, running from the chapel, westward to the south wall.

The smartest and most talented men served as gunners and cannoneers. They knew how and when to load and fire, made sure the right ammunition was used, estimated the distance from the target, and made sure the cannon had proper elevation. Gregorio Esparza, with Bonham and Almeron Dickenson, took charge of the cannon on top of the chapel, where Bowie lay helpless on his cot. Crockett was ready with loaded pistols, but he kept his Bowie knife close by.

The Texans fought so well that the Mexicans fell back. Some groups had lost half their men. The Texans danced and cheered at their small victory. They were sure that they could fight off the next attack too. The women and children hugged each other, happy they were not hurt.

The Mexican officers worried that a second try would not work if they did not attack quickly. They knew that help for the Texans could be coming soon.

The bugles sounded. The second assault began. But no ladder would stay in place long enough for the Mexicans to climb it. As soon as a Mexican soldier's head was up over the wall, he was looking down the barrel of a rifle. He would instantly be shot down, taking the ladder with him.

Again the Mexicans turned and fled. To the south, where Crockett was, they were able to get a ladder in place, and for a moment it looked as if they might climb it. Hundreds of their men lay dead or dying. Nerves were at a breaking point. They had to come up with a new plan in a hurry.

There would be four attack columns, three on the north end and one on the south. The attack plan called for the Alamo to be hit on all sides. Romero came against the northeast, Cos against the west, Duque head-on against the north, and Morales against the south.

The attacking columns on the north end of the Alamo were hit with rifle, musket, and cannon fire. The Mexican soldiers were held up there but they did not fall back.

They reorganized and kept going. The south column, under Colonel Morales, was made up of various Mexican battalions. Their job was to keep the defenders on the south end busy while the other three columns made the main assault. Morales moved his men and took the southwest corner. They got into the Alamo at the northwest corner by General Cos' men. Romero's and Duque's columns came later at different points along the north wall.

On the third and last assault, Santa Anna put in extra men with the battery to the northeast. Under the new plan, the weight of numbers would force them through the opening in the north wall. Others tried the ladders, and this time they got into the Alamo from the west.

Travis, on the north cannon, was shot through the head, but he did not die before taking a Mexican officer with him. Without fire from his cannon, the Mexicans flooded the north. The Mexicans were careful inside the Alamo. They dropped to their knees to fire or took cover behind pieces of wall.

Fearing for his life, Enrique Esparza hid himself in a pile of hay. Another young boy who was by his side put a blanket around his shoulders when the Mexican troops came into the chapel and killed the boy.

With the enemy at hand and at point-blank range, the Texans had no time or space in which to load their guns. Fighting became hand-to-hand, bayonet against sword, and shotgun to tomahawk.

A few Texans stayed at the cannon stations to blast away their enemies in the courtyard. But the Mexican gunmen shot them, one by one. The defenders began to go into the chapel, bolting the doors behind them.

Two Mexican officers put Santa Anna's flag on top of the Alamo, but not before they were shot by Alamo defenders.

Crockett died outside near the stockade wall, where

he and his "Tennessee Boys" fought. With him were nine-teen fallen enemies.

In a room on the chapel's south side, Almeron Dickenson, Gregorio's fellow cannoneer, rushed in to kiss his wife Susannah. He told her to do whatever she could to save their fifteen-month-old daughter, if she lived.

The Mexican soldiers found Bowie pale and helpless in the chapel. They lifted his sickly body with a bayonet and threw it to the floor.

On that day, March 6, 1836, Gregorio Esparza was hit by a cannon ball in his chest, while his wife and children watched. Ana screamed and tried to help her husband, but Santa Anna's men ran through the burning, smoky chapel to put an end to the defenders.

Santa Anna came to look at what he had done. Five men who tried to get away were caught and brought to the general. As he had said, there would be no prisoners taken. When he saw captives, he had them shot. Others tried to jump over the walls during the battle, but the same thing happened to them.

The battle had lasted thirteen days, and for Santa Anna and Mexico, the victory was complete. Not a single Texas soldier lived. The chapel mission was surrounded by American dead, who went down fighting.

While counting the dead, the troops found the women and children locked in the front of the building. They were kept there while guards watched them until daylight. Then they were moved to the Musquiz home to be questioned by Santa Anna.

The women and children were Mrs. Juana Navarro Asbury and her child, her sister Gertrudes Navarro, Mrs. Concepcion Losoya, her daughter and two sons, Victoriana de Salina and her three young daughters, Mrs. Almeron Dickenson and her baby (once believed to have been the only survivors — thus nicknamed "The Babe of the Alamo"), an old woman named Petra Gonzales, a teenaged girl named Trinidad Saucedo, and Antonio Fuentes.

After asking questions of the women at the Alamo, Santa Anna gave each of them a blanket and two silver dollars. They were set free to start new lives. None of them or their children would forget the bloody battle that had just ended.

Sometime later, Francisco went to his commander and asked Santa Anna if he could look through the dead for his brother. Santa Anna let him search. Francisco found his brother. Gregorio was buried at the San Fernando Campo Santo.

Mayor Francisco Ruiz counted the bodies of the other dead Alamo defenders. Santa Anna had them burned in two pyres. The smoke hung over the small town, filling the spirits and mind of those who survived.

Almost a year later, on February 12, 1837, Juan Seguin would locate the remains of the other men and have them buried near the funeral pyres.

CHAPTER FOUR

The Esparzas After the Alamo

The years after the battle at the Alamo were hard. Ana worked as a housekeeper and sold tamales to make money for her family. She was now mother to three sons fathered by Gregorio and two daughters from an earlier marriage to Victor de Castro: Dorthea Casarez Castro and Maria Jesus Casarez Castro.

Ana could not afford much. The one thing she wanted for herself was a buffalo rug that her employer had. She said she would work for free until she paid for it. Ana died December 12, 1847.

Enrique worked as a stable boy. Sometimes he took the leftover corn home to his family for food. He did not go to school. Like many frontier children, he never had the chance to live the life of a child. As a young man he had property on Nogalitos Street in San Antonio.

Between 1850 and 1860, Enrique, Manuel, and their youngest brother Francisco filed for the right to land in Atascosa County near Pleasanton, Texas, for their father's service at the Alamo. They had a hard time getting it, but they eventually received 160 acres each facing Galvan Creek.

The Esparza brothers were hard workers. They ranched, farmed a little, and ran a freight line between San Antonio and the coast. They also cut and sold fire-wood for people to use in their houses. They kept the money they made in a tobacco sack. Most of the goods they sold were grown and raised on their farms: corn, potatoes, butter, milk, beans, and meat.

Descendants say Enrique and Manuel were more alike. They both enjoyed history and were lifelong De-mocrats. All of the family were strong Constitutionalists.

Enrique

Enrique and a few other men split post oak trees with wedge and hatchet to build his four-room home. The shingles were also made of post oak. A kitchen was behind the main building. A rail fence went around the house and cattle pens on the ten acres. The floor was hard-packed mud.

On February 28, 1859, Enrique registered his cattle brand in Atascosa County. The brand was a simple "EA."

After the American Civil War in the mid-1860s, Enrique's land was worth only $200.

Enrique got into the freighting business. As goods carriers, several men would get together and form trains. Each had an ox-cart and two or three pair of oxen. Carri-ers moved goods in Mexican *carretas* pulled by huge, slow oxen. They lived in the *carretas* on the road as they would a house. Loaded with cotton and other supplies, they traveled to Port Lavaca and Indianola.

On these long trips the men would have all kinds of trouble. Sometimes the men and their animals would get sick. During the rainy season, the carts would cut deep holes until the narrow trails were not passable. The men would have to sit and wait for the sun to dry the ground so they could travel.

Freighting became one of the first money-making

businesses in San Antonio. Freighting masters had to be brave, tough, and honest. They hauled all kinds of goods, from staples to silver. Freighters faced Indians, robbers, rough roads, short water supply, broken wagon wheels, and sudden changes in Texas weather.

The first place Enrique went after his trips was to church to give thanks for his safe return.

Enrique married Gertrudes Hernandez, a widow, on May 13, 1850. Their surviving children were Maria Claudio Esparza, Micaela Esparza, Gertrudes Esparza, Apolonia Esparza, and Victor Esparza. Enrique and Gertrudes lost two children in 1861: Juana Ana, five, and Candido Enrique, three.

Maria Claudio was the first Mexican-American woman to enter the French religious Order of the Sisters of Charity of the Incarnate Word, on January 4, 1871, at San Fernando. This Order started the Santa Rosa Hospital and Incarnate Word College in San Antonio. Sister M. Claude served forty-three years, until her death on February 16, 1914.

Victor traveled with his father on many trips.

A very religious man, one of the first things Enrique did after moving his family to Atascosa County was to build a small church. Using common things, such as small rocks, slabs and mortar, he and his brothers built the church on five acres of land that Enrique gave for that use. St. (San) Augustine, the patron saint of the Sisters of Charity of the Incarnate Word, was picked as the patron saint of the little family church.

Since Enrique never went to school as a child, he studied from his children's books when he grew up. Educating himself, he learned to read and write. He loved to read and became a very good translator of English to Spanish, from print to spoken language, and vice versa.

In 1897, Enrique moved back to San Antonio and three years later to Losoya, Texas, to live with the family

Enrique Esparza

Enrique's daughter-in-law, Martina Esparza, Victor's second wife.

Sisters of Charity of the Incarnate Word. Enrique's daughter, Sister Claude, is first on left.

32

of his son, Victor. A good farmer, Enrique worked a truck garden on Nogalitas Street, between the Southern Pacific railroad track and the San Pedro Creek. Every morning he was up before daybreak filling the wagon with fresh produce to sell uptown at market. He and Victor were very successful at running the beautiful five-acre garden.

Enrique was the most well known of Gregorio's sons around San Antonio because of what he remembered about what happened at the Alamo battle.

He was firm-stepped and clear-minded in his old age, and told the most interesting story, a straight story. As he told what happened at the Alamo, his voice broke and he couldn't go on. While he could speak the English language, he spoke in Spanish:

"All of the others are dead. I, alone, live of they who were within the Alamo when it fell. There is none other left now to tell the story, and when I go to my last slumber, there will be no one left to tell.

"You ask me, do I remember it. I tell you, yes. It is burned into my brain and indelibly seared there. Neither age nor infirmity could make me forget, for the scene was one of such horror that it could never be forgotten by anyone who witnessed its incidents."

Enrique made several trips to Austin to see his father's name on the monument on the State Capitol grounds.

Enrique died on December 20, 1917, at eighty-nine, in Losoya. He had sold his land to his daughters, Apolonia and Gertrudes. He is buried in El Carmen Cemetery.

Manuel

Manuel owned a general store in Pleasanton. His home served as the store. It was built of stones and adobe and had dirt floors. The walls were plastered and white-washed, and even the steps were white. Cooking was done in the fireplace of the long kitchen in the back, which also served as their eating area. There were no windows in the room and little light came inside. Manuel's grandchildren would come to hate eating in the dark room.

In the store he sold coffee, sugar, and flour brought from San Antonio. There were no paths and the main road was far away.

At the farm he grew beans and corn and raised cows and sheep. Manuel registered his brand on May 27, 1863. The brand was a "P" with a mark across the stem.

On September 7, 1853, he married the great-granddaughter of Canary Islander Juan Leal Goraz, Melchora Leal, at San Fernando church. They had eleven surviving children carrying the Esparza name into the twentieth century: Petra Esparza Valdez, Melchora Esparza Bonilla, Juana Esparza Huizar, Ana Esparza Rodriguez, Maria de Jesus Esparza Montez, Simona Esparza Rodriguez, Isabel Esparza Huizar, Clemente Esparza, Elifonso Esparza, Manuel Esparza, and Gregorio Esparza.

Indian raids were still a very real threat to the Esparzas in Atascosa County.

One day as the children played and Melchora milked the cows, a group of Lipan Apache appeared on the other side of the bank. Melchora gathered and hid the children, telling them to be quiet. After a long wait, the Indians left.

In 1864, Manuel joined the Confederate army during the Civil War. He signed up for one year. Manuel had a rifle and stayed nineteen days at $2 a day. He and other farmers helped the South until their surrender.

During wartime, the wives and older men took care of the families left behind. The women plowed and hoed the fields. There was a shortage of nearly everything, even basic things. Pants and shirts were patched and then repatched.

After the war, the Carpetbaggers were corrupt and

Manuel Esparza

*Manuel's wife, Melchora
Leal Esparza.*

35

Manuel's wife, Melchora, and son, Elifonso.

Manuel's children: Juana, Gregorio, and Petra.

Manuel's son, Clemente Esparza.

Manuel's daughter, Juanita, and her husband, Sefarino Huizar.

Manuel's daughter, Maria de Jesus, her husband Eloy Montez, and son Jose Maria.

Manuel's daughter, Isabel, with husband William Huizar.

Seated: Isabel (Manuel's daughter) and her children and some of their spouses: Matilda, Delia, Alice, Lena, Elias, Ben.

38

violent. Nearly every form of wealth was destroyed, but not the land. Between 1870 and 1880, the value of Manuel's farm doubled.

On August 15, 1886, at the age of fifty-six, Manuel died. He left behind a widow with eleven children. Melchora and some of the children lived in the house built by Manuel until 1920. Melchora died February 13, 1922, at the age of eighty-eight. The land and home were then left to their daughter, Melchora.

In 1926 the house was sold. As recently as 1950, much of it was still standing. When Manuel died the special relationship with the land between brothers ended. The sale of Enrique's property to his daughters in 1900 ended the original connections with the land.

Francisco

Francisco was three years old when his father died at the Alamo. He, like Manuel, was in the Confederate Cavalry during the Civil War under S. Ragsdale, who was all over the Southwest. Francisco later became a Texas Ranger.

He married Maria Petra Zamora on September 30, 1851. They were married by Parish Priest M. Calvo. Francisco and Petro had ten children: Elisio Esparza, Blas Esparza, Simona Esparza, Francisco Esparza, Maria de Jesus Esparza, Simona Esparza Villanueva, Crescencia Esparza Andrade, José Angel Esparza, and two whose names are unknown. Only four of these children lived to be counted on the 1900 Census records.

On November 26, 1860, Francisco sold his 160 acres of land in Atascosa County for $400. He left his wife and children.

About 1872, Francisco was living in Tucson, Pima County, Arizona. He had traveled the area with Ragsdale during the Civil War and liked it. With a second wife, Matilda V., he had four daughters: Margarita

Francisco Esparza as a Tucson, Arizona, marshal in 1882.

Esparza Maldonado, Juanita (Juana) Esparza Laos, Anita Esparza Aragon, and Francisca Esparza.

On May 8, 1873, Francisco became marshal in Tucson, Arizona Territory, and held the job until January 5, 1875, then again from February 23, 1875, until January 3, 1876. He proudly wore Police Badge No. 7. As a marshal in Tucson, he was called "Don Panchito."

Francisco was known for being a tough lawman. He policed an area called "The Wedge" in Tucson, which was a rough area in those days.

Francisco was deputy sheriff at the time of Tucson's only lynching on August 8, 1873.

Store owners Vicente and Librada Hernandez were killed by three men in a robbery. Reward money was put up to catch the men. Eventually all were found, and Francisco got a reward for their capture.

Tucson's citizens were angry about the murders. The prisoners were told about the town's mood. They asked the priest to pray for them. But in the end, townspeople became so angry that they killed the murderers. The police officers whose job it is to keep things like this from happening could not be found. None of them.

Francisco died of a sunstroke in Tucson, June 30, 1887. He was fifty-four years old.

A copy of an envelope from Margarita Esparza, postmarked Tucson, July 28, 1887, shows that Francisco's two families did know of each other. In the letter Margarita tells Blas how shocked and upset she was when their father died. "He was not used to the sun, and when he left, it was to die," she wrote. Margarita told how happy it made her to get letters from Blas and his family, and how much she wanted to see them. She told Blas that Francisco cared for his children in San Antonio and wanted to see and stay in touch with them, but said that because of his work, he didn't get a chance to. Matilda told Margarita to ask Blas to consider "all of that." Francisco's first wife, Petra, died in 1924, at ninety-four.

Gregorio Esparza's family has grown into many offspring, some whose names are other than Esparza. These ancestors take seriously the responsibility of preserving freedom as descendants of an Alamo defender.

CHAPTER FIVE

Church and School History

San Augustine Church

Many settlements were formed from the missions around the ranches and farms and at river crossings near San Antonio. The building of modern highways has left some so far out that they are almost unknown. Others have disappeared. Many of these communities had mission churches which were important in their day.

In 1869, Enrique and Gertrudes Esparza gave five acres to the Catholic bishop in Galveston so that a small chapel could be built near their home for family worship. Before this time, when people wanted their babies baptized, a priest from San Fernando would have to be summoned. Several babies would be baptized at the same visit. When a group of people got together in a home, the priest would say Mass.

The walls of San Augustine Church were built by making forms of slats, then filling them with native red rocks and mortar. At the east end of the building were two small rooms for the priest, a bedroom, and an office. The floor was square bricks. The altar, sacristy, and rooms of the priest were wooden. The post oak shingles for the roof were made by hand.

First San Fernando School class.

San Augustine Church.

The priest kept his horse and buggy in a stable some distance east of the church. He slept at the church and had his meals at Enrique's home.

Neighbors gave and cooked food for the priest and special visitors. The church members gave corn and feed for the priests' horses.

When the bishop came for confirmations, there was great excitement at San Augustine. The men of the parish rode horseback in pairs for several miles to meet him. Much rejoicing followed the confirmations. When the bishop left, the men also rode back to San Antonio with him.

The first baby baptized at San Augustine was Manuel and Melchora's daughter, Melchora Esparza, in 1870.

One celebration the church observed was the Feast of St. Isidor, held on March 15. St. Isidor is the patron saint of crops, farmers, and farming. The patches, orchards, and crops were blessed and first fruits given to the Lord on this day. After the ceremony and praying, there was dancing and fun.

On the Feast of St. John, June 24, Enrique got up early in the morning to go bathing. To celebrate the body and spirit, horseback riding was the favorite activity for men and women on this day. Both events were common in Spain and brought to the New World by Spanish *padres*.

The pageant of Los Pastores was an important part of the San Augustine worship. The cards and dialogue had been handed down from generation to generation.

The first church was struck by lightning in the 1890s and burned. The members rushed to repair it. Family legend has it that the first church became too small because the community was growing, so a larger church was built on the same site. The walls were made higher by adding red brick. Then a belfry was added to the church. The bells of San Augustine rang to announce Mass, births, and deaths. Each event was made known by a special signal and tone. Elifonso, son of Manuel and Melchora, was the church's official bell ringer.

Other churches were built in the area and soon there were not enough priests to supply the need. A priest no longer lived at San Augustine, but Gregorio and Elifonso Esparza traveled in a buggy to Gray Town and brought the priest to San Augustine to have services. Manuel's family lived near the church and the priest often stayed with them on weekends. Other neighbors offered their homes to the priest as well.

San Augustine served the people of its area for many years. The last service there was in 1940, when a storm ripped off the belfry and almost flattened the little church.

Only three outside walls were left by the late 1960s. The roof was gone and the inside gutted. Time was not kind to the church that was home to one of the first Sisters of the Sisters of Charity of the Incarnate Word, built with the hands of two men who were child survivors of the Battle of the Alamo.

The San Augustine School

A small *palisado* school building was built about the time of the building of the first church. The school was located just yards to the west of the church.

It was a twenty-by-thirty-foot, one-room school with two doors. One door centered on the west and the other on the south, near the southeast corner. There was one desk on the north side that was the length of the room. The seat was a long oak log split in half with oak pegs for legs. The floor was dirt, as in their homes.

The second building was a frame one. From the 1880s to about 1917, classes were taught by nuns. A shallow, twenty-foot deep, hand-dug well lined with rocks was used for water.

According to the 1870 census, all of the Esparza children went to school there.

First San Augustine School.

Second San Augustine School.

Third San Augustine School from the Esparza Ranch, circa 1946, pictured in 1985.

This school was replaced by a third frame building. Classes were held in this building until the 1950s, when they joined the Leming schools. According to one Esparza descendant, the building's last use was as a school for black children in Atascosa County.

Early Schooling

The plans the pioneers made for San Antonio's schools may have been the most important thing they did for the city. There was public education in San Antonio before 1836.

The first students to get an education were the Indians who lived around the early Texas missions. About 1760, the very first book written in Texas was used to teach the Indians. The friars' work was to educate and civilize them.

Education faced many problems during these early days. Outside the missions, a wandering schoolteacher took care of school matters. A Spaniard, Don Jose Francisco de la Mata, took pity on the youths of San Antonio and started a private school in San Antonio, sometime before 1789. It was located where City Hall now stands. In that year, de la Mata asked the city council for help in getting money for the school and for the right to discipline children without parents stopping him. The people of San Antonio were not too happy with this. De la Mata was up against some of the same problems faced by educators today.

Others came after de la Mata, but 100 years or so would pass before education would be taken seriously as an important part of San Antonio's growth. There was no money for schools. Mexican authorities knew the need for education, but most people were poor and it was hard to set up a school system.

The constitution of Coahulia y Texas stated that a "suitable number of primary schools" were to be started

49

for all towns in the state. In the early months of 1800, Governor José Francisco Ruiz made the parents of children send them to school or pay three *pesos*. In 1803, at the age of twenty-three, Ruiz became schoolmaster. He went to school in Spain, where he learned philosophy and religion. Classes were held at his home until 1810, when San Antonio's first school was built. The school was made of sand, stone, and adobe brick and cost the Spanish government 855 *pesos*. Sixty-five children under the age of twelve were allowed to go if they could pay the fee.

Students were put into groups of "able" and "less able." The "able" students paid a *peso* per month to go to school, while the "less able" ones paid four *reales* per month. Ruiz's salary was soon being paid by kind citizens. Some years it only totaled 200 *pesos*.

Paper, slates, and catechisms were the only school supplies needed. The state supplied these items to children whose parents could not pay for them. Books were priceless, since they had to be ordered from Mexico City or New Orleans.

Because people who lived on the frontier wanted to govern themselves, schools started, but many soon closed because there was no money to fund good teachers.

The next teacher after Ruiz was Francisco Barrera, who had been a teacher at San Fernando. He was not able to earn a living at teaching, so he also did public writing.

Don Ignacio was the next teacher, in 1820. He said that the children were given too much freedom and asked the government to pass a law to keep children off the streets and make the parents support the school.

San Antonio had to pay the teacher and keep up the school when they could afford it. The teacher lived in the schoolhouse. The average pay for a teacher would have been less than $1.30 a day. The state would not help. That meant parents of school-age children had to pay for it all. As a result, schools opened and then closed in the

1820s. Sometime later, the state Congress set aside land to support public schools in Texas.

The first state board of education controlled all school policy. Each community had charge of its own affairs and handled the money from the land it sold. This still forms the idea of the state system of education. What money the city made on cattle, they gave to keep the school going. Parents still had to pay, since profits from the cattle were few. Since the poor parents could not give what the richer ones could, the rich parents made up the difference, to make sure the schools stayed open. The wealthy didn't like paying more, so they had home schooling for their children or sent them away to a private school.

Running a school was very difficult. When the pay dropped to next to nothing, the teacher quit, leaving the students without a teacher. When school was in session, the smarter students helped the others in larger classes with one teacher over them all. This method, called the Lancasterian system, was very popular in Mexico. The subjects were very simple compared to today. The smarter students were taught a small amount of grammar in addition to the regular subjects. The others learned basic math, reading, and writing, the Catholic catechism, and a few civics lessons.

School was very serious to the early settlers of old San Antonio. It lasted most of the day and went year round. In summer the students went to school at 5:30 A.M., "books took up" at 6:00, and the morning session lasted until 11:00. Three hours were given for a recess and *siesta*. At 2:00 P.M. the students went back and finished their day. "Books let out" at 6:00 P.M. The only difference in the winter was that "books took up" and "let out" an hour later. The students were to call each other "citizen," and the teacher "*Señor*."

The school put the students into "reds" and "blues."

51

Those who wore blue were called the Romans, and those who wore red were called Carthagenians. Each group had a president, six captains, and corporals. These officers were responsible for the behavior of their members as well as the overall work of the group.

Tests were held on the first and third Saturdays of each month. Parents were invited to watch spelling bees and listen to speeches.

Students missed school often. Most boys and girls around the Alamo were needed in the fields or at the looms to help their poor families earn a living. That was the case for Gregorio Esparza. He never got an education. Gregorio could not read or write.

*O*n *a cool, starry night while the Esparza family rested in their home, there came footsteps at the doorway. Maria sprang to her husband's side and held his arm tight. Gregorio and his brothers also stood, startled.*

"Juan, it is Jose Navarro," the visitor announced himself. Juan opened the door suddenly. Standing before them, leaning down to peer inside, was Jose Antonio Navarro.

"May I speak with you, Juan, on a serious matter?"

"Sí, Jose. Come in, please."

"I am here to talk about your son," said Navarro.

"Which one?" Juan looked at them both.

"Gregorio," Navarro replied. Juan looked shocked. He knew his sons very well, and he knew Gregorio would never do anything wrong.

"I've watched him. He's a smart boy and a hard worker," Navarro continued. "He needs schooling, and not this on again off again system here. My nephew, schoolmaster Francisco Ruiz, and I talked about him. He should go to school in the United States."

Gregorio stood and looked at his parents. Maria wiped her hands on her dress while Juan shook his head.

"It is sinful, Jose, to covet and not to be happy with what God has blessed us with already," Maria said. "Gregorio is ours. He has us to love him, and his Papa and I need him to help us work. Can the United States do better by him than his own family?"

"He needs education, Maria. A good education," answered Navarro.

"We are plain people, Señor Navarro," said Juan. "Not like you. In such a far off place it is not the same as home, you understand. My son would be different."

"This may be his only chance to learn to read and write and speak other languages," insisted Navarro. Gregorio's eyes darted back and forth to follow each speaker.

"No!" proclaimed Juan to Jose Navarro, standing and pounding his fist upon the wooden table to show his dislike for Navarro's idea. "Gregorio's place is with us. I will teach my son the things my father, Jose, taught me. To live off of the land, planting, hunting, fishing. That is what he needs to know, not this book learning you speak of."

Navarro stood and sighed. Maria moved across the small room to show him out. Putting his hands on Gregorio's shoulder, he looked sorry. Gregorio's head hung low and when he blinked, tears fell.

Gregorio's hope of education would not be realized during his lifetime.

In a paper dated July 5, 1828, Jose Antonio Gama y Fonseca set up the first "public" school in San Antonio. The McClure school, near the cathedral, east of Military Plaza, was built for the growing white population and was under Mexican rule. The classes were held in Spanish for 150 children. There were eight Ward Schools for whites and three for black children. The city also had private schools for girls and boys, as well as church schools.

The German-English school, a high-class day school,

was a landmark. The German Casino Association funded the school. It was an old, established, two-story house with a wide hall dividing four large rooms. Another large room, down the hall, was used as a kitchen.

On the north side of Commerce Street, Julius Berends, who owned a bookstore in San Antonio, was principal. He also taught a class one hour each day. Berends never punished his boys physically, but used the students' honor and pride to keep them in line.

The need for a "system" of public education was seen at that time, and in 1838, President Mirabeau B. Lamar, "the Father of Education in Texas," set aside public lands for public schools in the state. The state passed a law that ordered the town to sell the public property within their town for setting up and keeping schools. The leftover land was to go back to the state to be used for the schools.

The first public schools in San Antonio were under the control of the county and city. After being separate, they came together in 1855 with three district trustees called the Board of Education for the Regulation of the People's Schools of the city of San Antonio.

Between 1865 and 1890, several schools were built and the first superintendent was hired. He was a German named Plagge. The second school superintendent in San Antonio was W. C. Rote. He is remembered for having brought together a system of public schools and in 1879 having started a senior high school. Rote served as superintendent from 1879 to 1885. Under Superintendent J. E. Smith, the public schools were the pride of the city. Smith served two separate terms as superintendent of the public school system in San Antonio.

By 1900, San Antonio was known all over the state for its system of education. For more than 200 years, San Antonio has been the leading educational center of the Southwest. Millions of dollars have been spent on equipment and school buildings. Thousands of students come to San Antonio each year for schooling.

Mirabeau B. Lamar

An artist's rendering of Gregorio Esparza and family at the Siege of the Alamo, 1836. Purchased by the Culebra Park Community for the school.

Gregorio Esparza Elementary School

As educational leaders who have made a name for themselves throughout the country, Gregorio Esparza Accelerated Elementary School is blazing trails for others to follow. Located in northwest San Antonio, on the southern edge of the Northside Independent School District, the school community is committed to the Accelerated School philosophy. A dynamic, enriched learning environment is offered to all students.

Since the population of the school community has mainly been Hispanic, in 1972 the Culebra Park Community asked the school district to name the new school for a Hispanic figure. After discussion, study, and research, Gregorio Esparza was chosen as the school's namesake.

In 1990, the school did a study of the life, culture,

and background of Gregorio Esparza and Texas in the early 1800s. Units were written for each grade level, a school song was composed, and a pageant was produced showing Esparza's life and his role in Texas history.

Making their students aware of the privilege and responsibility of education is paramount to the faculty and staff at the school named in honor of Gregorio. These teachers saw a need for a vision for their students. In the Esparza School pledge, students promise to take their education seriously.

Each spring, during the week of Gregorio's birthday, the school bearing his name celebrates his life by teaching its students about the rich history that is theirs through Gregorio Esparza.

Faculty of Esparza Elementary School, 1994.

Esparza Pledge

I pledge to accelerate my mind and my actions to always excel in all of my academic and social endeavors.

I will cultivate a desire to learn.

I will learn the necessary skills to achieve my goals.

I will demonstrate the knowledge I have learned by realizing my goals.

I will always remember that I am responsible for my life.

I am prepared to take full responsibility for all of my actions.

I am truly a unique and wonderful person. . .

Because I am ME!

GLOSSARY

acequia: An irrigation ditch running along the center of the street.

adios: Goodbye.

adobe: A mud mixture formed into brick and dried in the sun; straw added to the clay mixture makes the bricks stronger and more waterproof.

alcalde: Mayor.

amigo: Friend.

atole: Ground corn mush.

barrio: A section of a town or city where the people are mostly Spanish-speaking.

bathing: A fancy place used for various forms of exercise and recreation.

bushel: 32 quarts.

Calle de los Adovitos: A street which led to the Villa de Nacogdoches in East Texas; now Nacogdoches Street.

Camino Viejo de las Carretas: Old Carts Road. Wooden wheeled vehicles covered with white cotton stretched over hoops; a covered wagon.

Campo Santo: Community cemetery.

Carpetbagger: A Northerner who went to the South during the Reconstruction period to take advantage of the poverty of Southerners. He came carrying his belongings in a carpetbag.

carretas: Huge wagons or carts.

catechism: A short book of religious beliefs.

chaos: Confusion, disorder.

confirmation: The ceremony of admitting a person to membership in a church.

descendant: A person born of a family.

entradas: Those who enter into a place.

epidemic: The spreading of a disease so quickly that many people have it at the same time.

expedition: A group of people that make a trip for a reason.

fiesta: A party or celebration.

garrison: Soldiers in a fort or town to defend it.

immigrant: A person coming from another country to live.

industry: Any business or trade.

integrate: To bring together.

Isleños: Descendants of Canary Islanders.

jacal: A Mexican hut with long, thin poles for walls filled in and plastered with mud.

lackey: A male servant.

Mestizo: A person of Native American descent.

monastery: A place where nuns or monks live by religious rules and vows.

Mulatto: First generation offspring of African-American and Caucasian mixture.

"no quarter": Term which means no prisoners will be taken; all captured will be killed.

padre: Father; title of a religious man.

palisado: A stake fence pointed up at the top and set firmly in the ground for enclosure or defense.

patron saint: The guardian saint of a place or person.

peso: Spanish dollar.

Plaza de la Islas: Main square; the homeland of the settlers that founded San Fernando de Bexar.

Presidio (de San Antonio): The military garrison of San Antonio.

pyre: A pile of wood for burning a dead body.

reales: Old silver coins representing monetary unit of Spain.

regimiento: City government.

sacristy: Place where sacred robes of the monastery are kept.

San Antonio de Valero: The Alamo mission.

secularize: To become worldly, rather than spiritual.

seize: To take hold of by force.

Señor: The way to adress a man; Sir.

Señora: The way to adress a married woman.

sentinel: A watcher or guard.

serape: A brightly colored wool blanket used as a garment.

siesta: A nap.

society: The people of a certain time or place.

solare: A land grant.

sombrero: A stiff, felt three-cornered hat cocked in sharp points with an upward brim and low crown.

summon: To request someone's presence; call for.

Tejano: A Texan of Mexican heritage.

Villa (de Bexar): Town of Bexar.

BIBLIOGRAPHY

Barnes, Charles Merrit. "Alamo's only Survivor Enrique Esparza Continues his Story of its Siege and Fall." *San Antonio Express*, Sunday Morning, May 18, 1907.

Bret, Officer Allan W. "Tucson Arizona Marshals and Police Chiefs."

Cervantes, Frances A. *Gregorio Esparza and the Hispanic Texans at the Alamo.*

Cobblestone, Volume 3, Number 3 (March 1982).

Coroner, William. *San Antonio de Bexar: A Guide and History.* San Antonio: Graphic Arts, 1890.

The Daily Express, May 1907.

The Daily Star, Sunday, July 3, 1887.

Daughters of the Republic of Texas Library. Alamo. "The Alamo and Other Missions of San Antonio, Texas."

————. "The First Cotton Mill in Texas was in 1740 in San Antonio."

————. "How San Antonio Schools Have Grown."

————. "Mission Life — San Fernando Cathedral."

————. "Papers Tell of First School."

————. "Prestige as School Center Dates Back Fully 200 Years."

————. "Schooling in San Antonio."

————. "Wandering Teacher Came Early to San Antonio."

Driggs, Howard R. and Sarah S. King. *Rise of the Lone Star.* New York: Frederick Stokes Co.

Eppinga, Jane. Volume 92. "Tucson's Only Lynching," 1991.

————. "Gunfighters and Lawmen," February 1994.

Esparza, Leal. *Atascosa County History.* Dallas: Taylor Publishing Co., 1984.

Franklin, Sammie. "Esparza Heritage Thrives in Atascosa County." *Pleasanton Express*, March 19, 1986.

"From a Texan's Scrapbook." *San Antonio Light,* October 29, 1950.

Glassford, Cora Carleton. "Gregorio Esparza A Hero of the Alamo."

Gomez, Art. "Historical Highlights, Handout #1."

Groneman, Bill. *Alamo Defenders.* Austin: Eakin Press, 1990.

Harris, Gertrude. "School System Here Begun Before 1789 by Francisco de la Mata." *San Antonio Express*, June 9, 1936.

Hindes, Kay Thompson. "A Historical Study and Archeological Notes on the Esparza Site: the Esparza Farms, the San Augustine School, with Relevant Character Histories and Biographical Information." San Antonio: UTSA.

Kerr, Rita. *The Immortal 32*. Austin: Eakin Press, 1981.

Lanier, Sidney. "San Antonio De Bexar." *Retrospects and Prospects.* New York: Charles Scribner's Sons, 1899.

"Last Survivor Alamo Dead." *San Antonio Express*, December 21, 1917.

Lord, Walter. *A Time to Stand*. New York: Harper & Row, 1961.

Mireles, Gerardo. "First Schoolmaster of San Antonio." *Texas Historian* May 1976.

"Mofi's History of Texas." *Texas Passages,* Fall 1987.

Poyo, Gerald F., and Gilberto M. Hinojosa, eds. *Tejano Origins in Eighteenth Century San Antonio.*

"Preserved At Museum San Antonio's First Public School." *San Antonio Evening News*, Wednesday, December 15, 1948.

Ramsdell, Charles. *San Antonio: A Historical and Pictorial Guide*. Austin: The University of Texas Press, 1985.

"San Augustine Dedication." *Today's Catholic,* April 11, 1986.

Santos, Richard G. "San Antonio De Bexar 1 de Enero 1836." J. W. Knight, County Clerk of Bexar County.

Scobey Fireproof Storage Co. "San Antonio de Valero — The Alamo."

Tinkle, Lon. *The Valiant Few: Crisis At The Alamo*. New York: Macmillan Battle Books, 1964.

"The Story of Enrique Esparza." *San Antonio Express* Saturday, November 22, 1902.

Vasquez, James R. "Public Education was here before the Alamo," *San Antonio Light*, 1986.

Personal Interviews

Esparza, Nora. Various dates between September 1994 and April 1995, San Antonio, TX.

Esparza, Reynaldo. Various dates between September 1994 and April 1995, San Antonio, TX.

Olivares, Lena. January 7, 1995. Verdi, TX.

Collections Visited

Alamo, San Antonio, TX.

Daughters of the Republic of Texas Library, San Antonio, TX.

Esparza-Rodriquez Cemetery.

Longhorn Museum, Pleasanton, TX.

Marshall Public Library, Marshall, TX.

San Antonio Public Library System, San Antonio, TX.

University of Texas Institute of Texan Cultures, San Antonio, TX.

ABOUT THE AUTHOR

CAHNDICE SMITH MATTHEWS is a graduate of Sam Houston State University. She is a member of the International Reading Association, the Society for Accelerated Learning and Teaching, and Alpha Kappa Alpha Sorority, Inc., among others. Cahndice Matthews has previously been named as an Outstanding Young Woman of America. She has taught in public and private schools in Texas and Kentucky, including Gregorio Esparza Accelerated Elementary in San Antonio, Texas.

Her professional writing career began in 1993 with her first published work entitled "Big Mama's House." Much of the author's time is devoted to her husband and young son. Among the author's interests are reading, interior design, and enjoying various types of music.

ABOUT THE ILLUSTRATOR

YVONNE DILLEY-CRUZ is a native of Laredo, Texas. She became interested in art at an early age. As a student in commercial art, she realized that art was to become a major influence in her life.

She graduated from Texas A&I University, in Kingsville, Texas, with a bachelor of fine arts degree along with an all-level art certification.

Presently, Yvonne lives with her husband in San Antonio, Texas. She has been teaching elementary art at Gregorio Esparza Accelerated Elementary School for the past six years.